REMEMBER ME

The Civil War Letters of Lt. George Robinson
and His Son, Sgt. James F. Robinson,
of "The Glenn," Hamburg,
South Carolina

1861–1862

Edited by

Richard L. Beach

HERITAGE BOOKS
2012

HERITAGE BOOKS

AN IMPRINT OF HERITAGE BOOKS, INC.

Books, CDs, and more—Worldwide

For our listing of thousands of titles see our website
at
www.HeritageBooks.com

Published 2012 by
HERITAGE BOOKS, INC.
Publishing Division
100 Railroad Ave. #104
Westminster, Maryland 21157

International Standard Book Numbers
Paperbound: 978-1-55613-503-3
Clothbound: 978-0-7884-8413-1

To
Laura Beach
and
Bryan Edenfield
for helping make this book
a reality.

TABLE OF CONTENTS

5
THE BANK OF HAMBURG
5
SOUTH CAROLINA
FIVE
FIVE
Cash.
Pres.
American Bank Note Company

INTRODUCTION

Remember Me is a chronicle of the early months of the Civil War told in letters by Lt. George Robinson and his son, James Fraser Robinson. These letters give an unusual perspective into the daily life of both an officer and an enlisted man in the 1st and the 7th South Carolina Volunteers.

Whether this book is being read for historical research or for pleasure, the story these men leave behind will make a lasting impression. This story is very private in nature as the letters are written to inform and to comfort those loved ones at home who are concerned for their health and safety. As such, these men give the reader not only a glimpse of history from a first-hand point of view, but also the inner thoughts of both an officer and an enlisted man in one volume.

In order to establish the personalities and lifestyle of the Robinson family during this time in history, several articles from the personal Scrap Book of the family's next oldest son are included.

The Robinson family consists of George and Anna, parents, and their children, James, George Cox, John, Harry, Maude, Isabelle, Kate, and Carroll. They are listed on the Robinson Family page in more detail.

Lt. George Robinson was born in Annapolis Royal, Nova Scotia, on October 8, 1817, the son of British Capt. George Robinson and his wife, Lady Francis Cox.

After completing college, George moved to Augusta, Georgia, to work at the Bank of Augusta for Mr. James Fraser. He soon met and married Anna Matilda Carter.

George left the bank to start a wholesale merchandise business across the river in Hamburg, South Carolina, a thriving community that had been the railhead for the Charleston-Hamburg Railroad when it was still the world's longest railroad. In 1852, he purchased a new family home, "The Glenn".

Anna Matilda Carter Robinson, daughter of Dr. John Carter and Martha Milledge Flournoy, was born in Augusta, Georgia, on May 9, 1823.

James Fraser Robinson, nicknamed Jimmy, was born August 6, 1843 in Augusta, Georgia. He graduated from Richmond Academy, Augusta, Ga. Jimmy was 17 years old when he and his father joined the 1st South Carolina Volunteers in January 1861.

George Cox Robinson, the oldest son left home while his father and older brother were stationed in Charleston, was born December 11, 1847.

The other members of the family are mentioned in various places in the letters.

Lt. George Robinson and Sgt. James F. Robinson wrote letters to home from Charleston starting January 9, 1861. The last letter from Charleston is dated April 26, 1861. In these letters they describe their daily life while working to build the defenses in the Charleston harbor. Included are accounts of the firing on the *Star of the West* and the firing on Fort Sumter.

When his company was disbanded, George Robinson returned home to Hamburg to manage his business and farm. Jimmy enlisted in the 7th South Carolina Volunteers and was sent to Northern Virginia.

From Virginia, Jimmy tells of his surroundings and the life of a Confederate soldier. His letters here span from July 2, 1861, until his last letter dated August 17, 1862. In them Jimmy attempts to alleviate the concerns his family has for his health and safety.

The last letter is from Jimmy's commanding officer, H. W. Addison to George Robinson, informing him of Jimmy's death.

The background for the story that the letters tell is augmented by information from the Scrap Book of George Cox Robinson, the younger brother of Jimmy, who enlisted as a Confederate soldier in 1864 at the age of 16.

The Robinson Family Genealogies at the beginning of this book were written by George Cox Robinson. These give an insight to their family traditions and help to explain the importance of military duties as the Robinson family perceived them. The first of the two genealogies is interesting in the fact that he traces their relationship with the Lees of Virginia through his mother's family, especially since Gen. Robert E. Lee's mother was Ann Hill Carter.

The article which tells of "The Glenn" and of George Robinson's business interests is an excerpt from an article pasted in the Scrap Book.

James F. Robinson's obituary notice and the editorial tribute to him are pasted side by side along with two poems on one of the pages.

George Cox Robinson enjoyed poetry, having written several poems about his experiences in the war. His Scrap Book is a collection of newspaper clippings of family events as well as articles concerning Confederate Veterans, poetry, and pictures.

The letters of Lt. George Robinson and Sgt. James F. Robinson were carefully saved and protected by George Cox Robinson. Through him, this story has become part of his family's heritage.

After spending the last years of his life at the home of his daughter in Allendale, South Carolina, George Cox Robinson died in 1935. The letters and Scrap Book became the property of his daughter, Laura Mozelle Robinson Breeland.

Since then these items have been passed down two more generations in the same family. They are now being carefully preserved by one of Lt. George Robinson's great-great granddaughters.

It is with the help and encouragement of the descendants of Lt. Robinson that these letters and articles are now available in book form. Without giving up part of their heirlooms, they are interested in allowing them to be shared with all people who seek more knowledge of this part of our country's history.

Care has been taken not to change any of the spelling, capitalization, spacing, or punctuation. There are very few illegible words in the fifty-two letters, but where there are, the symbol [ ] is used. The reasoning for this is so that the authenticity and the original intent of the letters is not compromised.

Remember Me is a phrase that appears frequently in the letters of Lt. and Sgt. Robinson. It is but one of the many personal aspects of their letters that make their story one that the reader will find hard to put down until the last page. Because of the haunting sound of this phrase, especially when realizing that it has been over 130 years since the letters were written, this title was chosen.

Richard L. Beach
March 1991

ROBINSON FAMILY HISTORY

The Robinson Family

Parents

Father: George Robinson
Born October 8, 1817
Died July 13, 1869

Mother: Anna Matilda Carter Robinson
Born May 9, 1823
Died July 17, 1896

Children

James Fraser Robinson
Born August 6, 1843
Died September 13, 1862

George Cox Robinson - see below
Born December 11, 1847
Died April 7, 1935

John Carter Robinson
Born July 30, 1857
Died July 23, 1919

Carroll Robinson
  Born January 11, 1860
  Died March 29, 1894

Harry Carter Robinson

Anna Maude Robinson

Isabelle Fraser Robinson

Kate Butler Robinson

Virginia Carter Robinson

George Cox Robinson

Confederate Army History

Enlisted   -   186
Company   -   Troup B
Regiment   -   2nd Batalion Georgia Calvary
Paroled   -   June, 1865

Genealogy

Father's Name - George Robinson, born at Anapolis Royal, Novascotis.
Mother's Maiden Name - Anna Matilda Carter, born at Augusta, Georgia.

George Cox Robinson - Born of the above union, December 11, 1847, at Hamburg South Carolina.
Son - George Robinson
   Married   Of this union, Gertrude Howard Robinson
Rosalie Howard Vincent

Daughter - Laura Moselle Robinson
                     Laura Robinson Breeland
   Married   Of this union
                     William Henry Breeland, Jr.
William Henry Breeland,M.d.,Phr.G.

In Re George Cox Robinson

My Father was the son of Captain George Robinson of the Sixtieth (60) Rifle Brigaede of England, whose Colonel was the Duke ofKent, Queen Victoria's Father. CaptainGeorge Robinson's Mother was Lady Frances Cox of Rutlandshire, England.

My Mother's Father was Dr. John Carter, the son of Robert Carter, known as King Carter, of Carotoman, on the Rapahannok River in Virginia. My Mother's Mother was Martha Milledge Flournoy daughter of Major General Tom Flournoy, Son of the Count Gustave Flournoy, a Huguenot, who settled in Tennesee.

On my fathers side there is no American connection other than our immediate family, on my mothers side the following families:

Mother's Father

Carters	of	Carotoman	Virginia
Lees	of	Shirley	Virginia
Nelsons	of	Yorktown	Virginia
Pages	of	Pagebrook	Virginia
Hopkins	of	Winchester	Virginia
Byrds	of	Winchester	Virginia
Burwells			

Mother's Mother

Flournoys of West Virginia & Tenn.
Henrys of Tennessee

History of the Robinson Family

The first Robinson followed William The Conquerer of England, and distinguished himself as a chevalier, so much so that William The Conquerer gave him a tract of land in Yorkshire, England, Known as "Oakland". This property is still in the hands of the Robinson family.

xiv

One of the Robinsons accompained Penn to America and helped to found the State of Pennsylvania. The Robinsons occupied a good social position in the county, so much so that George Robinson, (the ancestor) married Lady Frances Cox or Rutlandshire, England. He was Captain of the Sixtieth Rifles, known to the world as The Royal Brigade of England, the most distinguished organization in the British Army. He followed the fortunes of the regiment through a number of campaigns. At the Battle of New Orleans he carried Lord Peckingham off the fields. The regiment was ordered from America to reinforce Wellington in Belgium, and fought in the battle of Rennes, and next in the battle of Waterloo. After the battle of Waterloo the regiment followed Napolean to Paris. From there they were ordered to Nova Scotia, where Captain Robinson's wife, Lady Frances Cox, gave birth to a son, and died. This baby was named George Robinson. After he graduated from college he went as a protebe to Mr. James Fraser, who was president of the Bank of Augusta, Georgia. He entered into commercial business there, and finally moved to Hamburg. While in Augusta as a young man he married Miss Anna Matilda Carter, the granddaughter of General Thomas Flournoy of the French nobility. Their son and oldest child, James Fraser Robinson, was killed in the Battle of Maryland Heights, in 1862. His sister, Virginia Carter Robinson, married a Mr. Hill and died while a bride. Other children of George Robinson were: George Cox Robinson, born December 11, 1847; Isabelle Fraser Robinson; Katie Butler Robinson; John Carter Robinson, Carol Robinson, Anna Maude Robinson, and Harry Carter Robinson.

Brief History of the Carter Family

The Carter family of Virginia are decendants of John Carter, a colonial officer who settled in Augusta, Georgia, after the Revolutionary War. His brother, Charles Carter, married Anna Hill of "Shirley" (the grandparents of General Robert E. Lee).

John Carter married Lady Betty Langdon of Gretnall, England, and this was the beginning of the Carter family. Their son was known as Robert "King" Carter.

An excerpt from a newspaper clipping in the Scrap Book of George Cox Robinson.

THE GLENN

..."The Glenn" was purchased in 1852 by Mr. George Robinson, who was in those days one of, if not the largest, merchants doing business in the one-time thriving town of Hamburg. Mr. Robinson's business was an extensive one, he selling goods to merchants as far away as Athens, Georgia, and other distant cities and towns. In after years, however, on the waning of the brightness of Hamburg as a business center, Mr. Robinson moved his business interests to the city where he became associated with the firm of Fleming & Rowland, wholesale grocers, at No. 238 Broad Street.

Mr. Robinson was an Englishman. His father, Captain Robinson, fought under the Duke of Wellington. Captain Robinson was a captain in the Sixtieth Rifles, which regiment was commanded by the Duke of Kent, afterwards William III of England, and father of Queen Victoria.

The military instinct was handed down to two of the grandsons of Captain Robinson who served the Confederacy in the trying days of the 'sixties, James F. and Geo. Cox Robinson.

An excerpt from
the Scrap Book of
George Cox Robinson

Fairfax Station V
Sept 6 —

Rate 10

Mrs. G. E. Robinson
care
Mess Fleming & Rowland
Augusta
Ga

45

Private James R. Robinson
Comp. H, 7th Regt. G. C. v.

THE LETTERS OF
LT. GEORGE ROBINSON
AND
JAMES F. ROBINSON

Morris' Island April 5th 1861

Dear Mother-

This is the first chance I have had since I left home to write to you. You must not think that I forgot about the Ambrotipes. I asked Father so much about them that he got very mad with me. You must forgive me that I did not get it taken. But the very first time that I can go to Charleston I will get mine and send it to you I will go for nothing else. I hope that you will not be worried about it for you do no know how much it bothers me. I think that I may get a chance to go soon. We are encamped all together in tents

turn over-

LETTERS FROM CHARLESTON

Dear Anna

I am well and so is Jim and in good spirits - excitement runs high - we have just recd our arms, fine ones - been under arms ever since - slept on Steamer *Excel* last night - on wharf now waiting to go to Moultrie - expect a fuss to night - had one this morning - they drove the cutters out - write to Nelson Carter - God bless you all

Jany 9/61   Geo Robinson

not one Moment to Spare

-/-/-/-/-/-/-/-/-/-

Dear Mother,   Fort Moultrie, Jany 10th/61

I hope this will find you well. Father and my self is well. You must excuse my short letter for ever thing is confusion here, we are doing as well as we could expect. Please write soon and direct to care of Capt W. Spires. Father is very

3

anious to hear from you
> Your most affectionate son,

> J. F. Robinson

Dear Anna

We slept in our clothes ever since I left home - all excitement here - Food & water at first scarce - but now plenty - we are under orders to retire out of the range of Sumpters Guns on the first fire - leaving every thing but our Blankets - we are expecting it every minute - All in good spirits. write me to Charleston - Care Capt W. Spires Charleston - All Communication between us and the City may be Cut off by Sumpter's Guns - Write me every day - God bless my children & you, I am now writing 6 1/2 o'clock 11 Jany - Jimmy hand me his letter last night he has a good room nearly behind mine, and has a good mess with him - Henry Key and I room together - we have 500 men now in the Moultrie house and the wings - the wings are not so much Exposed as the main House to the Guns - Good Bye. Jimmy & Myself send every love to you -

> Ever Your Husband

we are in the wings
> Geo Robinson

and quiet comfortable If I live to get home - I will make you all laugh. remember me to Jolly

-/-/-/-/-/-/-/-/-/-

Jimmy is a Corporal all well - Kiss my little ones - and God bless you all - I dont fear any fuss damn them - let them come

> Geo.

Jany 14, 1861

I am just off drill and no Steamer we have good times - but expect every moment a turn - Jimmy commanded a squad just now and did it very well - I should say damn well - we have had some leave - Hansom Butler & 2 [   ] - dont talk about it - so mortifying - I am gaining laurels in my Company - I dont want to come or go home until all is settled - take good care of yourselves - and tell old Jolly the men tell me if I live to see Hamburg they will Carry me on their Shoulders or draw me in a carriage we will not be taken prisoner - you need not hunt Yankee prisons for us - kiss Bella & Kattie - Johnny & Carrol - and tell them daddy thinks of them every day and sheds many a tear no one sees but the great Supreme George & Jimmy look after every thing at Home - I have seen N. Carter twice - but no time to talk much - very polite - I am now writing on my knees - on my trunk - expecting to hear - a dam Chalk Face - Say - Lieut - come - Capt of the day wants you

Geo

-/-/-/-/-/-/-/-/-/-

Fort Moultrie Jany 61

Dear Mother

I received your letter yesterday. You cannot gues the pleasure it gave me. Father went to Charleston for it. We have had a few persons to desert us before we was sworne in. And I do not want You to believe one word they say. for we are as comfortable as we can wish. I am as happy as a jay bird. tell Wash that I say I can beat him cooking. O for a plate of Your biscuits and butter, is what I say every day.

Our Company has had a very bad beginning. when we stopt at Granateville John Hard had his company drawn up to salute us as we past in fireing the canon it burst and wounded two men. When we got to Charleston we was stationed on board the steamer *Excel*. On the morning of Wenesday 9th Jany we heard the fireing of big guns we all crowded on deck to see or hear. after a while a steamer came from the scene of action loader with soldiers. we soon learnt that the Steamer, *Star of the West*, attempted to land at Fort Sumter. but being fired upon she turned her back and went to sea. they say the balls hit her and that is all I know about it. You know better that we the news from Washington. We do not know what they do even in Charleston except when one of us go there. You have heard about Toombs & Scott. But I must tell you what happened to us. when we went to the Arsenal for our guns, we had to march close to a hole in the floor of the Arsenal used to draw up boxes. when the Cherokee ponds company went to pass they crowded so much that they pushed one poor fellow down. and I hear that he has died from the fall. We are stationed in the Moultrie house You know that we have a splended place for drill or parade. they are working on Fort Moultrie night and day. tell George that a Rooster is in danger here but in Charleston I saw some royal ones. I have not seen a pretty Girl since I left home. kiss them all for me and tell them that I am safe. excuse my poor writing and spelling.

Your most faithful Son

J.F. Robinson

-/-/-/-/-/-/-/-/-/-

Charleston Jany 18, 1860

Dear Anna

I am now in the City until 4 this eve - Jimmy & self Both well - recd another letter Yesterday & papers from you - Sent one to Jimmy the other a 5 pages written in the Guard Room - Hope you recd it - I would give the world to see you - Last before going to Bed - I looked thru my trunk, and behold the Bibles - I wept over mine before leaving this morning, I told Jimmy to go to my trunk and look at it - we will not disgrace you or it - Col Gregg is the Best Officer on the ground - not a Tyrant, But a Strict Officer - I like him very much - he is very Polite to me - I do my duty - I sent 2 to the Guard House last night - I am strict to the letter. we are now expecting soon to attack Sumpter they are making all arrangements for it - are 1100 strong - and will be placed out of the range of the Guns - and run not the least risk, except they attempt a landing - and that is not looked for - any how - I shall do my Best - I intended to have sent some fruit up to day - But was sent down to Buy Shoes, Shirts and a number of things for the Company - But the money the Co was not enough - and used mine - our company had nearly 800 dollars in Cash at the Fort I will get returned when back at the Island - I have to Economise until I receive pay - as the First 2 days we had to look to ourselves in a great measure - we never have suffered - never did. Soldiers have such Quarters, I sleep on 2 Mattr - - and all have good room & Beds plenty of Plain Food - William Dortie sent me a fine Roast Turkey - thank him for me - will write soon to him - But have to pick my time - Kiss all for me - and may God take care of you -

Geo Robinson
Your Husband

-/-/-/-/-/-/-/-

7

Fort Moultrie Jany 19th 61

Dear Mother

I have received yours and sisters letters. I am very sorry to see that you have placed any confidence in the tales that you have heard from those that deserted us. to show you how we fare I will mention what we had for dinner the other day. Father received from Mr Dortic a roast Turkey and sauce. I dined with him and Capt Spires. Yesterday Father went to Charleston, while he was there Capt Spire received a box containing a roast Turkey. Pies Cakes & C and I was kindly invited to dine with him. our dailey fare is better than most of Company has at home. We are all satisfied and comfortable. We have been received and Col Gregg has been placed over us. he is not Wm Gregg of Granateville who was beat in the election by James Carrol, but a perfect gentleman and soldier. Father and my self would be perfectly happy if we could hear that you was so do not think that we are suffering in the least. We will receive in a few days our Uniform. which will be of a gray color. cap Jacket. Pantaloon and over coat with a cape regular military stile. our company is getting along finely we have two cadets who drill us. We drill four times a day and a dress parade. We see the Commander but once a day. Father was the Officer of the day the other day. our company is increasing every day. We received a member from Alabama who came here to join us. You know what splendid sights we have every day you can see vessels of all sizes from the large ship that croses the sea to the small pilot boat. Tell George that if he was here he could learn how to build boats better than he can now. When we was stationed in Charleston there was lying close to us a Ship from Nova Scotia. and we use to watch the sailors by the hours mounting and splicing the ropes they would go so high that they would look no larger than a monkie and we would expect them to fall every moment. Tell Sister that it is a lovely sight to watch the waves as they come dashing in and to follow them when they retreat And at night when I sit

8

in my room and think about you all I can hear the call of the sentinel and the dashing of the waves. I do not room or mess with Father he has to mess with the Officers. Among my mess is P. O. Ransom. Wallace Delph Casper Gardner. and others. Some of those who ran away from us has returned and I wish you would tell me in your next letter what they said and how they was received. the Abberville company you spoke about is in the same Regiment that we are wich is the 1st Regiment of Voluntiers. You must excuse me for not writing more but William Barber is going to Charleston and he will carry it for me he is waiting for it now

Your most Obedient Son

J. F. Robinson

-/-/-/-/-/-/-/-/-

Sullivans Island Jany 24th/61

Dear Mother.

I received your box a day or so ago. Father and my self are a thousand times oblidged to you for the nice things that you sent us. every person in my mess told me send you their best respects. In my last letter I forgot to tell Bell and Kate of the Shells that I gathered for them. last Sunday I and some others went to look for them We had a delightful walk of about five miles on the beach. You know the old saying (that every dog has his day) and I believe my day is coming. Capt Spires you know appointed me 2nd Corporal. Mr Scott got a discharge from Col Gregg and that raised me to the 1st Corporal. I will tell you something that hapened to me the other day. I was Corporal of the Guard and I had three posts to attend to. during the night a sentinel from a post which was not mine called but the Corporal not coming after waiting a long time I went to him thinking it was my duty to do so. When I went up to him I found that he had stopt four drunken men who had not the countersign. I told him to keep them there untill I went for the Captain of the Guard when he came he took them to their rooms. In the morning I found that they had broaken in to a respectable mans house and shot at his daughter. Col Gregg was very mad about it and sent them to the Guard house. He will try them by a Court marshall tomorrow. Yesterday Col. Gregg sent for me and another Corporal to come to his house. I thought it was about the drunken men but it was about another thing both of us got off safe. He treated us like a perfect Gentleman Father and all the officers that I hear speak about him says they like him very much. You know I told you that we was stationed in the Moultrie house. our rooms did not have any fireplace in them. Father went to Col Gregg to see if he could not rent a house close by. He said that he could do so and that the state would pay for it. Father got a nice house with five rooms a fireplace and a kitchen in it is Father Mefs Welborn and Delph Wallace Delph and my self with a cook. We are as comforable as if we was at home. Tell George that Father says that it will not be long before he sends for him. Father will write tomorrow I have so much to tell you that I do know wich to tell first. Tell Sister and George that I want them to write to me. You must excuse my poor writing and spelling. write soon.

Your most obedient Son

J. F. Robinson

P.S. Please direct your letters care of Capt Spires Sullivans Island

J.F.R.

Dear Anna

We have moved in Comfortable Quarters, and would be quiet at Home, but there is always a confounded set of Pirates belonging to all Companies - and may have to move - I shall to Morrow, - Kiss my Bella Kattie - Johnny & Hug-Kiss Carrol - and see if he would look round for Daddy - do you think he would remember me - I would give a heap to see them - I shall write Georgy to Morrow - also Ginny soon - she writes to my satisfaction Fully - I may in the coarse of 2 or 3 weeks see you all - but I dread the Parting again - dont send us anything - Keep Everything for Yourselves -

Yours always
Dear Anna
Geo. R

-/-/-/-/-/-/-/-

Sulivans Island Feby 6/61

Dear Mother

I received a letter from Gus. Glover yesterday in wich he tells me that the river is very high and all over Hamburg, that explanes why we have received a letter from you for one week. Father has and is very anxious about you all. He goes for a letter every time the boat comes over and he says that you are sick and will not write because you know it will worry him, but I told him to wait and he would find out the reason why. Please write as soon and as often as you can. We are all well and kicking

Yours Truley

J. F. Robinson

-/-/-/-/-/-/-/-

11

Sulivans Island Feby 7/61

Dear Mother

We received this morning a number of letters from Yourself, Sister, and George. We are glad to learn that you are all well and happy. We are in the same state.

If you could only look into our camp you would not for a moment think that we was here for the purpose of fighting but for pleasure. this is at night in the day it is a diferent scene. in some parts of the camp you can hear the fiddle and noise of the dancers. Last night some of the Boys found a sentinel a sleep in his box wich is put there for his use in wet weather they fastened him in and carried the box down on the beach. They try the Sentinels every way to get the countersign from them, and many a fine joke they have by some of them letting it out. Tell George that If Father goes home he will bring him back with him Tell him also that there is a pair of Roosters next door and they fight very often. Father has got his uniform wich is diferent from the Privates, Corporals and Sargents his is blue and looks beautiful. Mine will be gray. I told you a one of my letters that it would be a roundabout wich is a misstake it will be a frock coat. We learn by the news papers that Col Hayne has left Washington for home so we will know in a few days if we have to fight or not. We are ready and prepared. The commander of Fort Moultrie says he can stand the fire from Fort Sumter for a week. And Mr Charley Lamar says that it is impossible for Fort Sumter to knock down the Batterys on Morris' Island. Mr. C. Lamar and Whatley Lamar staid with us the other night. We are all well and doing fine

Your most Obedient Son

James F. Robinson

12

-/-/-/-/-/-/-/-

Sulivans Island Feby 8th/60

Dear Mother
    We received Yours and Sisters letters of the 7th to day we have received all of your letters in a clump, the high waters kept the mail back, and that was the cause of our not receiving your letters in time, Mr R. J. Delph has got leave to go home for a short time. And it is doubtful wether Father can get leave to go or not. I hope the screw will not hurt John. Give my love to him and all the rest of the family. We are all well and in good spirits.

Your most Obedient Son
J. F. Robinson

P. S. F. C. Barber has resigned, The election will come off soon. And I will tell you the result in my next you must excuse my short letter, I must go and take (a hasty plate of Soup)

J. F. R.

-/-/-/-/-/-/-/-

Sulivans Island Sunday Feby 24/61

George
    Father arrived here yesterday He brought with him Sister's letter to me. And also his beautiful Sword so kindly present-

ed to him by the people of Hamburg. It is one of the finest in the Regiment. I am sorry to see that Father did not bring you with him. I would like you to be with me so much I do not think there is a bit of danger. But wait a while and I will get Father to send for you. I know you would like to be with us Weather we was living in Tents or not. You should have been here on Washington's birthday every Fort in the Harbour fired salutes even Fort Sumter and it was a beautiful sight to see first the flash then the smoke long before we could hear the report. You must excuse my poor writing for I am more used to the Musket than the Pen. Give my love to all of the family And tell John to keep his nose clean

Yours Truly
James F. Robinson

-/-/-/-/-/-/-/-/-/-

1861

Sullivans Island 3 March

Dear George

I recd your Kind letter some days ago - and answer it now, just as I leave for Pellicants Point where I have no chance to write - in Tent - without Pen, Ink or Paper - We return here Thursday morning again, write me here as usual as all letters will be sent to me - I hope Your Farm is improving daily and your out of nothing, for I am out of money but hope to paid off soon. I love to see you all. does Carrol look round for me, and how is Johnny, Bella & Kate I dont know I will see you - before this reaches you, we may have Fort Sumpter - we dont know anything about that more than you do and it may happen at any moment - and to Morrow is the 4th write me often - for I am very anxious. Jimmy is well, and leaves in the morning he is strong as a Buck I shall write Ginny next - I wrote to your Mother Yesterday - My Best love to all

Your Father
Geo Robinson

-/-/-/-/-/-/-/-

Morris Island Mar 14/61

Dearest Anna

We are now more easy in feeling, as the impression the Fort will be given up - we have worked night and day putting up Batteries - and they are fixing them so the U S Navy cant come in. If he dont come out in a few days - we will force him - any how we are to move soon again further up the Island - in Tents - we are not comfortable now about 90 men in one House and no quiet - not a stamp - paper & Envelopes out - But I shall go to Charleston shortly - as soon as I am paid off - but up to this time no one could leave, looking hourly for an attack - but I think now - everything of that kind will be outside - England and France wont allow their ships stopped - and we have the Yankees any how - Anderson is under the worst Features - nothing more than a Prisoner - Jimmy is well - and as soon as we can get out pay - and other matters work right I shall get him a furlough - we received Both Boxes - thank Kennedy for me - the first leasure and paper I will write him - we go to the Batteries from Morning till Night. this is our first idle morning 1/2 past 8 - God only Knows ten minutes ahead out next order - When at Pellican Point we ordered immediately to Morris Island not time to finish our dinner if we had our Tents - I prefer this Island to Sullivan's - I am afraid the Knats will be very bad - they are coming

15

already - our days are now hot and the nights very cold - I was Capt Guard the other Night - and found a big fire more than comfortable - our water is not as good. and much Better than lower down on the Island - we only have to dig a few feet and get good fresh water - little too deep it is Saltish - I am hearty - only don't like our arrangements - no chance to write - no place of private - but thank God I shall be in Tent soon and then it is my own - and no one shall intrude I am very plain Spoken to them Kiss my little ones and Write often love to all

Your Husband
G Robinson

-/-/-/-/-/-/-/-

Morris Island March 20 1861

Dear Anna

I have slept warm once this week - and that was Last night we received more Blankets yesterday this is queer climate - hot some days and almost freezing before day - Yesterday - snow was announced covering the ground - by good luck - we had a good house - We are allowed a servant to each officer - govt paying for him - we now have Hazard from Hamburg - and have Sent for another. we go into Tents shortly which will be more comfortable - we are too crowded - I shall send you 100 doll. by Express - I receive 158.50 in a few days - bor\d 40.00 when I went home leaving me 18.50 next 2 mos due again 2 April - you can depend regular for it be sure and tell George to be particular of all letters for they may contain money and he not Knowing it - when you get your money - pay Your state Taxes - and do the Best you can

16

I dont fear a fight - but have more fear of being shot accidentaly by the men - but thank God no Liquor will be allowed to Privates - except smuggled in - which will be hard to do - Jimmy is well - Ransom & John Harrison were refused a Furlough - I am going to Charleston as soon as paid Jimmy must have a Sergts sword & Belt - he will have 30.00 - next time 34.00 Corp 13 - Sergt 17.2 - Next time Sergt 34.00 he looks well and seems to enjoy himself exceedingly his wiskers show now - I hope you are getting along well - write me daily - we are doing as well as can be Expected - I dont think now we will have any difficulty - we are well Fortified - Big Guns in Batteries all along the Island - no Fruit this year - it is a great loss I was in hopes it would have yielded a small amot at least - If the Fort Sumpter is given up - I dont think I will have any difficulty in getting Jimmy a Furlough - I will try any how by the 1st April - I would love to see you all it is 6 o'clock in the morning sun shining in our windows 14 Dressing & washing - and Big fair to be a fine day - but when it is cold & rainy - so exposed no protection - but summer is coming - out of 1100 men - only 3 reported Sick slightly - Gregg says it is beyond belief Kiss my little ones - and every love to you and all

Your Husband
Geo Robinson

-/-/-/-/-/-/-/-

Morris' Island March 22nd/61

Dear Mother

I received your letter this morning I am sorry to learn that you did not get my letters regular for I wrote almost every other day. Our Company has all of their uniforms except their caps. The Coat and Pants is of a gray color. With a black stripe down the leg of the pants. The Company turned out to drill this morning and they did as well as the Regular's. Col Gregg told all of the Captains that Fort Sumter would be given up Sunday. It is opinion of all that this Regiment would be disbanded in a few Weeks. Some of the Soldiers left Fort Sumter yesterday Lieut Welborn was down at Cumming's Point and saw them when they left for Charles ton. We are stationed about three miles above Cummings' Point and about a half a mile above the Star of the West battery. Our House being too crowded we got three tents from the Quarter master in one of them is Wallace and William Delph, John Harrison and my self In another is P. O. Ransom, T. C. Tompkins, John Lyons, John Perrice and Casper Gardner I prefer living in tents. They are warmer than the house and not as noisey. I am not tyard of a Soldier's life but will be glad to get a chance of seeing you all wonse more. Kiss all of the Children for me tell them that Father and I are well.

Your Son
J. F. Robinson

-/-/-/-/-/-/-

Dear Anna

    I sent by mail to Jimmy lost one Stamp, I send my Carpet Bag By Mr. Finch - have my clothes washed, and returned by him - dont Send any Fannels back - as the weather is now getting warm - Send my other draws and Socks - if he dont return in a week mark - on a Card - Lt Geo Robinson Morris Island - send by Express and pay for it - I can get along 8

18

more days without it. I have one clean Shirt left - Jimmy has all his - I will try one of his if Short - nothing new - we expect Wednesday to have the Fort - But that report has come so often - we dont beleive it - and only will, when we get in - I am told - Matters are arranged except the Military Form of giving it up - our Beauregard intends to make him come out, not with honor take good care of yourself - write daily love to all

Your Husband Geo Robinson

March 25/61
Morris Island

-/-/-/-/-/-/-/-/-

Morris Island April 1st 1861

Dear Anna
    I am now writing in a tent having moved further up the Island - Capt Spires' & my Tent - have not yet come they are called Wall Tents much larger than the Soldiers - only 2 officers in one of them - when 4 privates go in a much smaller one - The wind has been blowing very hard for the last two days, and every thing is covered with a light Sand - our food - indeed every thing is covered with it - We are now building a Kitchen - indeed it is a good one - and since Jimmy Left we have changed our Messes - Capt Spires Myself - Henry Key & Welborn - Geo & W Kemaphan - John King & Jimmy are in my mess we had on the other Island small messes - but Since on moving to this - we have been thrown together until now - every thing in a few days will be comfortable - You no doubt was surprised and pleased on seeing Jimmy - I sent you more money than I once wrote you pay my State Taxes

19

and let my City taxes stand - find out who is the proper
person to receipt it - dont pay without a receipt - as for my
City Tax I will be at home before the 1st May, and will ar-
range - I hope you enjoyed the Fruit - I will try and find some
again, when I have money - on the 8 May if we stay that long
we will Paid again - every 2 mos - I am writing uncomfortable
- but will write soon again - You will get this soon after
Jimmy leaves - Kiss my little ones and best Love to all
Your Husband Geo Robinson

I dont Know what the State Taxes are, but have written to
Hamburg to know - pay it what ever they are
GR

-/-/-/-/-/-/-/-/-

Morris Island April 4, 1861

My Dearest Wife

I met Jimmy yesterday morning at the Pavilion Hotel in
Charleston I having gone over the day before - I took tea with
Nelson Carter - I like him - he is a plain nice Gentleman, his
wife, no Soul - may suit him - but time must have gone that -
In crossing from Charleston to Morris' Island our Batteries
opened on a Yankee Schooner - and made her leave - tho the
Shooting was Bad - that's twice Jimmy and I have been
caught under Sumpters Guns - Anderson sent over to our
Island and wished to Know why the vessel was Fired into -
The Answer was - we were ordered to do it - the messenger -
observed if she is hit - the Tea Party opens to night - we know
not what an hour brings forth - Beauregard has notifyed our
government - Batteries all ready - to night Col Gregg has

20

returned from the City (he is a member of the convention) his orders are - all Furloughs to cease - those gone to the City to return at once - Something out we expect hourly to do something - all alone in my Tent - 10 o'clock at night - a lantern swinging close to my Bed - and a candle on my Trunk - Wind blowing almost a Hurricane every Tent more or less loose - mine is a Small Soldiers Tent - Spires & myself each have a wall Tent but the wind so high cant Pitch them everything covered with Sand - but thank God, I am alone once more - that I may write you once again in Peace - Jimmy is Sergt of the Guard - Comfortable in a good House. I have changed messes - 4 Officers & 4 men - I picked Jimmy - we comfortable so far - and his Tent mates are nice men - W Sale made me a present of a camp Bedstead - it is very Comfortable - Lt Welborn and myself will be bed Fellows - he is going to purchase one for his use Tent Fellows not Bed - for only can sleep in them - Key Tents with Spires - we changed on Spires a/c - Key wont let the men impose on him nor I either - Spires & Welborn are good natured I keep my Tent clear - and Key Spires' - I Built a good wooden Kitchen - my energy had it Built - I wont let anyone but our mess use it - ever since I have been on this cursed Island until now - we occupied one House 90 men - and there was no quiet I told them when I got my Tent I would Show them - I had one of our men "Nolan" from Augusta Drummed out of the Company - and will push things further than that - Hearty as a Buck been Sleeping in the sand - you would be pleased to look in at me - close by the Sea - Continual roar wind, Sand & water - alone amongst 1500 men - thats strange, but true - on the eve no doubt of some great change - some dambling - some drinking - but I am alone with thee and my God - absent but not Forgotten - never that - Sleeping or awake - I am enjoying the quiet luxury alone - alone - thinking of thee and ours - our darlings - and may the God of Battles protect you and our little ones - let it come I am tired of this delay - we are ready - things must come to close soon - Wigfall made a stir-

21

ring Speech in the City Yesterday - all the Charleston Cos are ordered here and to Sullivans - The Damn Yankees will find no childs play - they will never attempt to land troops - but Anderson may return our fire - it is universally believed we will open on him in a day or two - but no one can tell - rumors are many - you will Know as soon as it happens - My lamp swing so - by the Tent shaking I can hardly write - Kiss every one of the children for me and if I live until next month, I will come - or send you some more money - anyhow - all my soul is with you this night - when all is quiet in my Tent except my heart - it is troubled - and far from here - and the Tempest out side makes it feel strange - at this moment my Tent Made a lurch I thought it was gone - I just straighented the uprights if it goes my Kitchen is close by - I will gather a Banket and sleep there - do the Best you can - dont be afraid I will send you all I get - Money aint any use here except to pay for washing - which aint much and 5 to 10 cents a day for the daily Papers let George push the Farming - make all the Plunder you can - no Peaches - great loss - How did you think Jimmy looked - let me all your thoughts - I got him a good Sword not one equal to it in the regiment
God Bless you all

Your Husband
Geo Robinson

I had to Finish - my candle is sinking in the Lantern
2.00 enclosed Buy some candy & cakes for the little ones

-/-/-/-/-/-/-

Morris Island April 5th 1861

Dear Mother
    This is the first chance I have had since I left home to write to you. You must not think that I forgot about the

Abrotipes. I asked Father so much about them that he got very mad with me. You must forgive me that I did not get it taken. But the very first time that I can go to Charleston I will get mine and send it to you I will go for nothing else. I hope that you will not be worried about it for you do no know how much it bothers me. I think that I may get a chance to go soon. We are encamped all to gether in tents I was put on Guard as soon as I got here. I have just got off I found every thing right and going on smoothly We are all well and comfortable They have not yet stoped Major Anderson's supplies There was a small Vessel that tryed to come in the Harbor with the United States Flag flying but we sent her out a flying it proved to be a Vessel owned in Charleston. I here no talk about disbanding the Regiment. But we all expect to stay our full time out. They all seamed very glad to see me. You must give my best respects to some young ladies you know who I mean. Tell Sister that she must play Dixiey's land once more for me. The Abrotipes shall surely come.

Your most obedient son
J. F. Robinson

-/-/-/-/-/-/-/-

Sunday Eve April 7, 1861

Dear Anna

I am now writing in my fine large new Tent - almost as comfortable as if in a house - The weather has been exceedingly wet and windy - no comfort - but now it has the appearance of clearing off - Yesterday I was laying on my Bed reading Harper for March about 5 o'clock, enjoying the quiet - raining outside in torrents with high wind - but I was safe & dry - when in comes the orderly from the Col - Co G H& I appear by 6 o'clock at Col Lee's Battery one hour for Supper - our Co G - and the others went - worked until about 9 - Wet to the Skin - I ordered our Co to quarters - expected to get a reprimand - but didn't - Anderson's supply from the City Cut off - he may stop the Steamers going to Charleston from our quarters - If so - we commence on him at once - 50 Sharp Shooters from our Rifle Cos have been ordered to Cummings Point (that is on our Island, and nearest to Sumpter) - to take off his Gunners - we have shot into their vessels twice and he has not returned it - he may not do anything about his provisions being cut off - but you know by our Working in the night in one of the Worst Storms I ever saw that we are on the alert - I had on my Big White over Coat and my common every day clothes, and my Glaze Cap - and was drenched - now I am dressed in a full Soldiers uniform like Jimmy's - pants fit but coat make for a short man the pants I shall Keep - would the coat also - if near fitted - dont cost any thing - my uniform cap is a beauty - to morrow I am Officer of the Guard - turn out in full uniform - Jimmy is well and in good Spirits if communication is cut off (it cant be altogether) - but mails will be more irregular, as they will have to be sent long ways round - but write often - I wrote a long letter to you a few days ago - Sent 2.00 for Candy - let me Know if you got it - also about all your affairs - Box of Fruit - money matters and all - if I live until 8 next month I shall send you another sum - all I can - But it is great Satisfaction to hear from you - the Draws you sent me, came in good time - I have not changed, but will soon. I lost my Blacking, and just found it - my servant came in to Black my Boots - and I had to stop to Hunt it - was in a cursed Bad Humor thinking some Damn Rascal had stole it - my tent is the quiet - only Welborn and myself - he Laughing at me - they steal from him so regular - he says he cant help Laughing - but my

24

Blacking is now here - Kiss the little ones. My ears Burnt at 12 - I thought of you all at that time - and felt Sad.

Your Husband
Geo R

-/-/-/-/-/-/-/-/-

Thursday Morning 6 o'clock
April 11, 1861

Dear Anna

We are here yet and no Yankees - <u>news</u> <u>always</u> now <u>exciting</u>. Glad of it. - it makes them prepare better, and more on the alert - troops arriving daily - I write merely a few Lines - because you are hearing contradictory news - and I know when you see my Hand writing - you know things are right - God Bless you all

Geo

Write often, if only 2 Lines

-/-/-/-/-/-/-/-/-

Saturday 12 - 1862

Dearest Anna

We opened Fire on Sumpter Friday Morning, and Saturday at 2 o'clock ([ ] Time) he gave up - Saturday morning about 9 we sett Fire to his Barracks inside the Fort - with Hot - <u>Red</u>

Hot Balls - The Firing commenced at 4 o'clock in the morning - 6 Large War Steamers laid in Sight off the Bar - We were under Arms most of the time - and last night we were behind the Hills - raining and Blustering - looking every moment for the enemy to land. but we were strong - It was a beautiful Sight to see the Red Shot & shell passing to and fro all night - when the inside caught Fire - the Red flame spread rapidly - Black Smoke - Bombs bursting in - and Shot flying in made it look wild - we soon get accustomed to such things.

To night Saturday - all the Steamers knocking round - and dreading the Yankee tricks. we are ordered to sleep in our clothes and our arms by our side - they may make an attack - and share watch closely - Rockets going up - You must have Known we were in for it by not hearing daily from me, for I always write even ever so little when things look Squally - all communication was cut off from the City by Anderson - except far round - Did you get 2.00 in a letter - I have not heard from you lately - but may.to morrow - neither Jimmy or myself felt any fear - laying down at night in a blanket on the sand with between 2 & 3 thousand men in our neighborhood also watching - but may thoughts were Home - My darlings - every thing in life was there - no throb except for them - laughing & Jesting - but Oh God - how I longed to have you more comfortable - and this same night - when men are moving thro the Hills on the look out - not knowing when and where the blow shall come - How sad - when I think of you all - but I am determined to make them Know that we are and always will be free - to a morrow - I shall give you more about the night - and if not - this that I leave unfinished will show you my last - my greatest love is for you and my darling children - Kiss them for me - because when you get this - I shall be one thing or the other - If I finish and direct - then all is well - but if another has to send it - you will Know and no suspense - Write me let me Know if you have heard anything about and how - at this hour the

Boys are laughing & Jesting and expect at any moment to meet in deadly strife - such is life - Bless you - Good night.

1/2 past Five Sunday - went down to the Steam Boat - Col. Heywoods Regt from Barnwell just arrived Gus Haywood one of the Soldiers - beautiful morning - Sumpter looks Black & lonesome - cant find out till nine this morning - steamers laying off the Bar - made no move during the night - Blockading our Harbor - But Cotton is King - now for Coffee - Shoulders & white oak splits - Jimmy well on Guard all night - accustomed to it - can sleep on top of Rail Fence.

The Mail leaves
We have the Fort
G R

-/-/-/-/-/-/-

Morris Island April 14th 1861

My Dear Mother

I have just received your letter of the 10th in which you tell me of quite an exiting time. I shall tell of Better and more glorious News it is the (Taking of Fort Sumter) for we have the above Fort in our possession and what is better not a man killed on our side. We took the Fort in a fight of Thirty hours. On the morning of the 11th a large Fleet appeared on the bar and in the Evening of the same day we demanded the surrender of the Fort. Major Anderson stoutly refused and said that he only had supplies for four days but that he would not give it up untill he was forced to do it At half past four next morning the firing began it was splendid I shall never forget the sight. We began the fight and he returned it promptly. We began by throwing Shells in to the Fort it continued all that Day and Night The plan was that the Artillery was to fight him while we kept Forces from being landing from the Fleet and we expected they would try it every moment. At Night we slept on the bare ground and the Rain was awfull We had Sentries along the Beach for five miles. We slept with our guns loading and by our side. I say slept but you know that their was not much sleep in the rain and the firing going on. On the morning of the 13th about ten O. clock the Fort all of a sudden took fire from our hot balls and shells The sight was magnificent the bright glare of the flame and the darkness of the smoke. Then we began to fire faster. You see where the Shells bursted and tell by the brick-dust where the Balls hit. first a chimney would go and then a part of the walls or a gun dismounted. Notwithstanding the fire and the Balls Anderson would keep on firing First on Fort Moultrie or Fort Johnson and then turn his attention to Morris Island. The Iron Battery stood the fire well and every shot from it told. Two guns in the Iron Battery was dismounted not by Anderson's balls but by the severe shocks caused by shooting. such is their force. About 1 Oclock P. M. a Shell (I think) from Fort Moultrie cut down the Flag staff. And you ought to have heard our shouts The Fireing kept on for about a hour longer When he sent a boat over with a White Flag And Fort Sumter was taken which was two days before impregnable. Fort Sumter is hurt terribly, large holes through it. all the wood-work burnt down. Every Barbette gun is dismounted. While Fort Sumter was burning and we was fireing in to it. The United States Fleet consisting of seven or eight vessels Stood the whole time about two miles from and in full sight of the Conflict. All our Officers who have resigned from the United States Army or Navy have cursed them. I hear that Major Anderson and Capt Forster will resign. They say that they will not serve with such arrant cowards. who will look on and see their brother soldier whipted and not attempt to assist him. Fort Moultrie have not escaped all together unhurt all of her Barracks was shot away But not a gun dismounted. Two large canon balls went trough Gen Ripley's private rooms I think that Fort Moultrie under the command of Gen Ripley did the most damage to Fort Sumter. The Floating Battery was placed at the nearest point to Fort Sumter from Sulivan's Island. she did her duty well And the Shells that she threw in to Fort Sumter was not a few. I do not think that she was hurt atall. I have not heard wether many of Anderson's men was hurt or not. The Fleet is here yet but I think they will leave soon. We have tried ever way to get them to come in but they will not. Our Flag has been presented and we thought that it would have been riddled by the balls before this but it has not had the good luck yet. We are all well and in good spirits. Do not worry yourself about us For the Yankees will not come near enough to shoot us.

Your most obediend Son
James F. Robinson

Dear Anna

I had to finish your Letter in a hurry - the Fort is ours - all communications was cut off until today your letter was recd dated 10th - My letter was dated Wrong - Fight commenced 12th

GR

-/-/-/-/-/-/-

God Bless you all Kiss all for me
Oh that I could see you
Morris Island April 16/61
Dear Anna

I received your letter this eve addressed to Jimmy - all's well - and am rejoiced to hear all's well - I was astonished to see Mr Kemaphen and Mr Schiller they are both here - Jim Holland was on the Island - but I was under arms - and could not leave my company - I was in a few Hundred feet of him, and could not leave my post - war regulations are very strict - I was on Duty all last night - it rained very hard, but I was under shelter - our whole Company are out to night except the old Guard who were out yesterday - the night clear

The War steamers are out of Sight, but dont fool us - we watch as well as Pray - they dare not land - the cowards would not help Anderson - let them try it - many a Blue skin will never see Yankee Land again - Last night when on Guard duty - You would have Laughed to have entered the Guard Room Hour 1/2 past 12 - Col. Gregg enters - Robinson - Capt of Guard 30 men under Him - Raining very hard - all enjoying themselves - I was sitting on a Keg of powder 3 others on cartridges on Kegs of powder in the centre a Keg of powder with a candle Burning and we playing 7 up - he walked in - looked round - gave orders - about lights out in camp - smiled and left us - no one cared a damn about him - It is said here - that Gregg's Regt dont care about anything - I can say - during the Fight - expecting the fleet to land 3000 troops every Hour - no one changed their usual occupation, some Lounging, others playing cards - some dice, some cussing - and the Sounds of Cannon for 30 Hours was neglected - except once in a while - Hurrah for Ripley - he is giving Anderson Hell or there goes the Iron Battery - or by God - we are getting Iron but when I <u>cried</u> the Fort is a Fire - (for I was the First saw it in our Quarters) - then Ripley commenced throwing 10 times as Fast his Shell and Hot Shot - up to that time - they were taking their time, making a Business of it - But then excitement ran High - flag at 1/2 mast for the Fleet to help him and if they had not have been worse than cowards they would have attempted to land on our Island and taken our Batteries But that would have amused them somewhat - Prudence to a damn Yankee, is the Better Part of Valor - they let him go - the Tea Party - They spoke of - came off - we opening the dance - and sending them the Invitation - mortifying when the Said a few days before they would give us one - we <u>can</u> and <u>will</u> make them

30

respect us - they dont come it - 75000 men - we will make them yet know, who has always Fought their Battles - they may come - and some of us may not get home - but at this hour 9 - at night - no one fears or care, and expect to sleep sound - Your young niger Baby I have hardly thoughts for - only glad - all's right who's [ ] You and my little ones all I care for now - tho it is a strange animal to our family - take good care of yourself - when we are in Danger - we think of Home - and [ ] those, who divide us from our beloved Homes - we will fight them with a Bitter Hate - and grasp them - with such a grasp - that many a one will wish he was at Home milking his <u>cows</u> - not Mexicans now - and they well know it

Your Husb
Geo

-/-/-/-/-/-/-

Charleston April 25/61

Dear Anna

I received Both letters yesterday - and can say little or nothing what will be done. We muster over 600 men in our Regt on Morris' Island - all well except bowel complaints. We are in hopes to be disbanded soon - we have bourn the whole burden, building batteries drawing cannon night & day - and the other Regts just arriving nothing to do - Some of the Kershaw Regt left last night for Virginia - we would not follow Gregg as Volunteers - our Best men are yet on the Island - Some good ones left - We don't like Gregg - and it was not right to make the demand on us to build Other Batteries and many causes too numerous to mention - I came over last eve and leave again for Morris Island at 4 o'clock this afternoon -

31

will write you every day - but so hope at the Next Pay day to be disbanded - that is 8th May - anyhow. I shall try and be right - love to all and kiss all for me.

Your Husband
Geo Robinson

-/-/-/-/-/-/-/-/-

Morris Island April 26/61

Dear Anna

I have just returned from Charleston, every thing quiet - it looks like Sunday, altho about 2000 men on the Island - no excitement building Batteries - or drawing Cannon - The Inn very hot and one feels languid - that naturally comes after great excitement, not a War ship in sight - they placed our fine Rifle Cannon, on the *Lady Davis* - one of our War steamers - the rifle is a present from a Carolinian in England to our state, and came just in time for the Battle of Sumpter - and did great service - I call it a beauty - Watch for me anytime shortly - I dont know when - but send down on Monday night or Tuesday next. We are trying to leave on Monday about 2 - get in Hamburg about 11 o'clock at night - but dont look too hard - as we are Military, and have to bide the time of our Superiors love to all - and devilish homesick

Your Husband
Geo Robinson

32

LETTERS FROM VIRGINIA

Fairfax C. H. Army of the Potomac
July 2nd 1861

Dear Father
I received your letter of the 22nd June a few days ago. I am glad to hear that all of the family are well. We are having a great time Encamped in a beautiful Country. where we can get any kind of fresh meat we wish. The best of water & wood. Fruit is just getting ripe here. Cherries are very plentiful and better that I ever saw before. I find a great difference between this and Morris Island. Guard is quite heavy. They are just beginning to put us to work. We are getting very strong here. Troops arrive every day. We have plenty of Artillery. I think this will be our Camp for some time. As they are digging trenches and planting canons. Gregg's Regt left this morning Gregg has been trying to get them to come back with him And some try to make out that they will come back. But I have been through their Camp. I found his Guard Tent full as usual. And the Prisoners abused him very much. Among the Prisoners was Blackwood Benson & old John Sikes. Blackwood said that Gregg was mad and put him under guard for spite. John Sikes asked very kindly how you was. I found by asking that the Regt will not come back with him. Gregg. But I think that he will get a new Regt

wich he will a call the 1st. Coming through Fairfax I saw Lieu Thomas of Gadberry's Comp. he told me to be sure and give his best respects to you. All of the Officers of the 1st ask very kindly of you. One more Company joined our Regt this day. Capt White They are from the Northern part of the State near N. C. I hear that more will join. Our Regt has now 1050 men and when the other's companies join we will have one of the largest Regts. Gus Glover & Charley Rodgers are both well. We have very little sickness in our Regt. Lieut Doxier has resigned on account of ill health. Milledge Weaver was elected in his place. I have not received a letter from Mother yet. I have received Sister's in wich she told me that Mother has written I will get it soon. Tell Sister that I will answer hers in a fews days. I am perfectly well dooing fine We take Prisoners every day I mean the Cavalry.

Your Son
J. F. Robinson

direct letters to
Manassas Junction Va

-/-/-/-/-/-/-/-

Fairfax C. H. Army of the Potomac
July 5th 1861

My own dear Mother

 I have just received your letter of June 28th You can not imagine the pleasure it gave me. I learnt by Sister's letter that you had wrote to me but I had not received it on account of you not knowing where to direct. I am sorry to see that you think that I need clothing. I have plenty of every thing. And close to a Village where I could buy if I did. When I read your letter's they carry me right home And I can see every member of the family. God bless you. I think that after reading one of your letters I could whip a doxen Yankee's. You have such controle over my feelings that you can bring me to tears or smiles just by the stroke of your Pen. I have not forgotten a certain young lady you speak of. I can not tell of any of our movements. Because it is against order's. I am living in great contrast to what I was on the Island. We hire a negro Cook who cooks and washes for us. We have fresh meat for dinner almost every day. Cherries here are the finest kind. The trees are as large as our Pines. We have both the Black and the Red. Gus Glover & Charley Rodgers are both perfectly well. I wish Father would tell Mifs Rodgers & Glover. We have very little sickness in our Regiment. We had a nother Company to join our Regt the other day. Troops arrive here every day. Please remember me to all of my friends and to the young Ladies. And not forget the one you say watch our pew in Church. I have good Officers who treat me very kindly. Gregg's Regt has left here for home. He has been trying to get them to come back. But I think they will not. We are encamped in beautiful Country. The Clover is knee deep and on it grase the finest of Horses and Cattle. There is a house close to our Camp where we buy Butter and Milk. The Butter is as yellow as Goshen and the Milk the Richest I ever saw. We pay 20 cts a pound for Butter, 5 cts a quart for Milk. Chickens 15 cts apeace, Lamb & Beef 8 cts. Kiss all of the dear children for me. Please write often. I love to hear from you. Direct your letters to Fairfax C. H. Va and I will be sure and get them.

Your own true Son

James F. Robinson

-/-/-/-/-/-/-/-

Fairfax C. H. Army of the Potomac
July 11th 1861

Dear Father

I received your letter of the 11th yesterday. We are at the same place yet. I cannot tell you what we are doing but you can guess. I have seen Tom Lamar & Dr. Twiggs. Lamar has a battery here. All things are going on right. We have every thing that a Soldier could wish. If your are on Picket and no provissions with you. All you have to do is to stept in to the first house and get it. My Mess is living finely we have Tables Benche's & Shelves. We cook in the Woods. We have a Negro to cook for us & a coop full of Chickens. We can buy fresh Meat of all kinds Butter Honey Milk & all kinds of Vegitables. We draw flour and get a old Lady to cook it for us. We took a Spy yesterday. He was with our Wagoners who told us about him. He was a young lad and had the appearance of a female. He bragged of being a Black Republican and was as saucy as you pleas. We sent him to head quarters. I wish you would tell Mr Rodgers that Charley is well. Gus Glover is in the same fix. I am afraid that you do not get my letters as I write as soon as I get yours. I have answered every letter that I have received. I never was in better health. I am perfectly satisfied. My Officers treat me very kindly. I think that Gus G has enough of the War aready. He is tyard of it all ready. You know how changeable he is. He says that if Stovall comes here he will join him. Charley R. stands it well and keeps in good spirits. I was on guard on the 4th I planely heard the guns fired in Washington and Alexander. We took no notice of the day or the firing except to double our pickets. Our Pickets are very bold they go some times within the lines of the Yankess's and take

Prisoners. This is our Mounted Picket our foot Picket is stationed in the day. but move to a different place at night. Dr Twiggs & Tom Lamar went scouting day before yesterday. I lent Dr. Twiggs my Rifle. He returned safely yesterday You need not be anxious about me at all. I am perfectly well Kiss all of the Children for me.

Your Son
J. F. Robinson

P. S. Please remember me to P. Fleming and Wallace Delph.

Yours
J. F. R.

-/-/-/-/-/-/-

Fairfax C. H. July 13th 1861

Dear Father

I received your letter of the 4th day before yesterday and yours of the 9th yesterday. I am sorry to see that you have not got my letters for I have answered every letter that I have received. I am glad to hear that Mother's Eye is better. And all of the family well. You all are very attentive and kind in sending me Cloths and I am very grateful for it. But I do not need them. We are just getting knapsacks and all of the clothes that I cannot carry on my my back will be sent either to Richmond or Home. I have got more clothes now than I can carry. We got our Uniforms yesterday. It is gray round about jackets. With green trimmings and stripe on the pants. I think that we will be paid soon as the Pay Rolls have been made out. I heard yesterday that Johnson and Patterson had a brush. Johnson had eighteen thousand (18.000) and Patterson thirty thousand (30.000) Patterson besides his superior force was strongly entrenched. Johnson advanced and sent him word to meet him but Patterson declined. But their Pickets meeting Johnson killed 50 and took some 40 or 50 prisoners. This is all rumor and I cannot say whether true or not. We expect a fight every night for the Yankee's has advanced and we have done the same. The distance between the Pickets is only about half a mile. I was on Picket yesterday. we saw what we took to be Yankees but they retreated. One of our Videtts saw eighteen and they ran from him, showing their courage. I cannot tell you much of our movements or how we are fixed. But Beauregard is at the head and you know all must be right. We have great confidence in Capt Bland. he understands his buisness. Gen Bonham & Col Bacon seems to have the same feeling for him and his company. for every time we expect an attack our company is out, We have badges so that we can tell each other. And every thing is going on right, so when we move we go but to Victory. Davis & Beauregard knows what they are about. Charley R & G Glover are both well, I never was in better health. Remember me to all of my friends and ac-quaintances. And kiss all of the Children for me My love to Mother and all of the family.

Your Son

J. F. Robinson

-/-/-/-/-/-/-

if you can send a few old papers I will be very much oblidged.
J. F. R.

Vienna Va. Aug 1st/61

Dear Mother,

I received your letter of the 18th yesterday. I gave Capt Bland his, he said he would answer it. I have not received a letter yet dated after the Battle. This makes the third I have wrote since the 21st. I think that the letters are detained for a short time somewhere's. Be not anxious for a moment. You cannot amagine the greatness of our Victory. My Regiment held the Entrenchments. We expected to be attacked every moment. We was in a very trying situation. We had to stand and be fired at without a chance to return it. We could here the shots of the Guns on the field of Battle. We stood the fire calmly and when we was ordered out of the Entrenchments to storm the Battery that had been shooting at us We gave three cheers. wich the Enemy herd three miles oft. We jumpted in to the Creek and waded through. When we reached the Camp of the Yankee's they had fled. They left almost every thing. Gen. Bonham's Brigade in my opinion deserves the highest praise for alacrity wich they stood every hardship. We left Fairfax in the morning without a bit of Provissions in our haversack We traveled all day under a burning sun, without any thing to eat. And at night when we stopt we slep as we stopt. without covering. And the next day only a few Crackers. We slep on the bare grown in the soaking Rain with out Blankets or any thing else. We did this cheerfully. Because we was ordered to do it. We had rather by far to have stood and been cut to peices that to have undergone the hardships we went through. When the Enemy left his Camp he did not have time to waste I can tell you. I got a Oil Cloth a Blanket lined a Canteen & Cup and a fine haversack to carry provissions in. Our Boys was greatly in need of somethings wich they got. In Centreville was a fine dinner spred. And in a Carriage close by was baskets of Champane. On the 23rd we was ordered to advance to Vienna a distance of fifteen miles. We went to Centrevill 3

39

1/2 miles, Where we stopt untill night. We marched all Night. It was the hardest night I ever spent. We had not slep for several nights before. Men fell out of the Ranks at every stopt unable to go any farther. My knapsack seamed to cut in to my shoulder's. And I would have stopt on the way but I thought we would have a fight when we got there. I went to sleep walking along. We got to Vienna about 8th Oclock next morning. I slep all of that day. right where I stopt. We are doing finc now. Gen Beauregard's compliments to all of the Troops engaged in the fight was read to the Regt this morning. Kiss all of the children for me. And tell George that I have a knife for him taken from the Yankee's (if I do not lose it) Gus Glover & Charley Rodgers are both well.

Your Son
James F. Robinson

-/-/-/-/-/-

Flint Hill Va Aug 29th 1861

My Dear Father

I received your letter of the 24th yesterday. I am sorry to see by your letter that you do not get mine. I write regular. I am also very sorry to hear of the Death of William Miller. I was well acquainted with him. Our men is some coming from and some going to the Hospital every day. Sickness in the Brigade is decreasing. There is some talk of fighting in Western Virginia. Except some skirmishing all is quiet here. Lieut Harrison told me that he had recd a letter from you. My Officer's treat me with the greatest of kindness. And I think that the 96 Riflemen can boast of having not only the hansomest but the best Officers in the Brigade. We have a brigade drill daily. Capt Warley is here as Aid to Col Cask. Mr Dargen who drilled our Company on the Island is here also. I wish you would tell me in your next letter wich of the Boy's from Hamburg is with A. P. Butler. Tell Mother and Sister not to forget to write to me sometimes. And George also They must excuse me for not answering them personally. But I write to one for all. I am well. I do not need any thing. God bless you all.

Your Son
James F. Robinson

-/-/-/-/-/-/-

Flint Hill Va September 1st 1861

My Dear Mother

I have received you kind letter of the twenty fifth Aug. And also George's of the fifteenth Aug. And a Paper of the 23rd from Father. I am glad to see by both of the letters that you are all well. But I am sory to see you all in such low spirits on account of me. When I am in such fine health. You said in your last that you thought that you might never read another letter from me. You must never think of that. When you know that I intend to come back and ride all the extra flesh oft the Horses. We are all doing fine now. Duty light and plenty to Eat. The sick of the Regiment is recovering fast and some come back every day. We have had very few cases of Typhoid Fever. There has only one died from our Company. We are encamped in a healthy place about half way between Fairfax and Vienna. There is no news stirring this morning. It is sunday we have an inspection of Arms at 9 O clock and a dress parade at 5 O clock in the Evening. And I take this oppitunity to write you a letter. You must not be the least uneasy about me. Tell Father that I do not need any thing. Lieut. Harrison told me the other day that if I did need any thing that I could get it without sending home for it. My Officers treat me with the greatest of kindness. Tell George that he must excuse me for not writing to him personally for I consider my letters to belong to the whole family. When Gus left here I did not think that he would go home or I would have sent a letter by him. I sent letters by Mr Goodwin and Capt Merriwether who promised to deliver them safe. I have not recd your letter sent by Maj. Welborn. I received George's letter yesterday. It was handed to me by a Gentleman who said that it was given to him at Richmond. But he did not know who. The letter was open when I got it. It did not look like it had been broken open. But rather like it had never been fastened. There might have been another letter put in it. Write me soon and tell me what Boys have come here with Pick. Butler. The two Mrs Bland came here and staid with us two or three days. There is quite a number of Carolina ladies here. And old Mr Ruffian is here sometimes. I am perfectly well and in good spirits. God bless you my dear Mother.

Your Son
James F. Robinson

-/-/-/-/-/-/-/-

I have plenty of Money. but I think that the letter will go best this way.

J.F.R.   Flint Hill. Va Sept 5th 1861

My Dear Brother
I have received your letter of the 15th Aug. Mothers of the 16th by Lieut Welborn. And Father's of the 29th Aug. I must

read them all over and commence answering the questions. I will answer yours first. You ask but two the first is, is it not cold in Virginia. The Weather is very changeable here. at present the Nights are cool, not cold. and the Days Hot. And your next question is, have I received your other letter. Yas I received it. and is happy to hear that you get on so well with your Chickens, I will commence with Mother's next. I will take up the letter of the 16th Aug. Mothers' first is about the Flannels, have I any. Plenty. go in my shirt sleaves. Second. do you get your Father's paper's regular. Sometimes, Third. did not your uniform get ruined in that trying march to Vienna. All most, Forth, Overcoat. do you need one and how can it reach you. I have my old one, I do not think it could reach me. Fith, Did you break your promise during those terribl three day's. What promise. If you mean Liquor I could have got any quantity. But did not take a drop. Sixth, Cant you see Carroll by the hair. I see every one of you. Seventh. Are you well. Yes I am in good health. This is the end of the letter of the 16th Aug. I will take up Mother's note wich came in Father's letter of the 29th, all 2 question First, Flannels again. I have plenty. Second. Did J Walker give you a bundle. I am afriad that he has lost it. Never send any by hand I do not get them. Third. Does Gus tell the truth about my hardships. He does not. I am living finely. I hope he will stay at home. He is of no service here. Question Forth. do you hear me you young scamp. Not quite mam. You are a little too far oft. Father only asks one. Do I need any thing. I do not. I have answered all questions. I love to receive and answer them, for I know that they are questions of Love. Dear Brother I am going to ask you to do me a favor. You must remember me to the Mifs Buckmaster's and the Mifs Neelys. Write me soon. I am in good health,

God bless you all
Your Brother
J. F. Robinson

-/-/-/-/-/-/-/-

Flint Hill Va. Sept 11th 61

My Dear Father

I have received your letter of the 5th Sept. I am glad to learn that all is well and that you are getting my letters regular once more. I have also received from you two packages of papers. You cannot amagine the pleasure they give me. We get very few papers here. You are right about the postage. I think that it is the safest way to send them. I am very sory to learn that Mother has been sick. And am glad that she is better. You are very kind in sending me the Box. I think that it will reach me. But do not send anymore. I do not need it. About the Over Coat. It would be of great use to me. I do not need one yet. Do not let it cost much. I think that I could carry it. If you was to send it by Express I think I would get it. Never send anything by hand. I do need Flannels. I have plenty of every thing. My Regt is increasing fast. There is no new cases of Sickness. And not abit of news stirring. We think that the next Battle will be in South Carolina, so look out for Butler. I have nothing to tell. you must excuse my short letter. Give my love to all. And kiss the children for me. And may God protect you all is the prayer of

Your Son
James F. Robinson

-/-/-/-/-/-/-/-

Va
Flint Hill Sept 23rd 1861

My Dear Mother

I have just returned from a journey to Fall's Church. I have rece'd the Box, your kind letter. And some from Father, and one from Sister. one from A. C. Glover. We started for Fall's Church Sunday morning Sept 14th 61. There was two Regiments from our Brigade. The 3rd Col William's. the 7th Col Bacon's S.C.V. The distance from Flint Hill to Fall's Church is Eight miles. Col Williams kept on to Monson's Hill two miles farther. We stopt in the Village. And was held as a reserve. Fall's Church is a small Village. But it has some beautiful Residences in it. We staid here Eight days. While we were here, I visited Monson's, Mason's and Upton's Hill's. And the Sights I saw were more lovely than any picture I ever saw. The road to Mason's was very difficult. But when I did reach the Hill out of Breath, The sight repaid me for all my trouble. The Sun was throwing his last rays on Earth. I was looking East, the sun setting behind me. And before me laid the beautiful Potomac. I could see one tall Steeple in Alexandria. And the Fortificasions on the Hills around it. And by looking to my left I could see the City of Washington. There stood the Capitol, the Dome and both Wings. I could see the river for miles. See the Boats going up and down. On Fort Ellsworth I could planely distinguish the Star's & Stripes. The View's from Monson's & Upton's are not as good as from Mason's. These hills are named after their owner's. From Monson's I could see the Dome of the Capitol only and the Steeple in Alexandria. Our Picketts is only about four hundred yards from the Hill. And only about three hundred yards between our Picketts and the Yankee's. From Monson I could planely see both Picketts. Every now and then they would fire on each other. I could see their long row's of tents. Oh, that I was an artist, that I could take that lovely scene, Was my first exclamation's on beholding it.

45

We left Fall's Church Sunday morning 22nd Sept. and reached here the Evening of the same day. On going to my tent the first thing I saw was the Box. It had come safe to hand. While I was absent. But some friends took care of it for me. I well knew what hand had marked the Lid. I soon opened it. The first thing was the letter and the Envelopes. I was soon deep in the contents of the letter. I then went into the woods to read it by myself. And like a weak mortal as I am I had to have a hearty Cry over it. I could tell every thing , each one put in. Father the Lobsters, Candles & C. Mother that splended Cake, fine Jellies Cordial, Pickels & C. And I knew well those small fingers that picked the Haws put in the Candy. And the black paw's with the big heart that made the Biscuits. Thanks to All, For such kindness. I have just commenad Enjoying the nice thing's the Box contains. I have received the papers sent by Father regular. I have received also Sister's letter. And one from Gus Glover. And two from Father. I have also to tell of the Death of another Rifleman. Ches. Ma Gee, he was on the Island in Capt. Adam's Company. We had quite a number to return, While we was at Fall's Church. Please remember me to Dr and Mrs. Yelder. Take care of your Eyes Dear Mother for my sake, And those headackes. Oh, that I could have them in place of you. Is my earnest wish. And if I should ever come back Capt. Porgy's name shall be read <u>again</u> and <u>again</u>. And old black Tom as familliar as Wash, Kiss all of the Dear Children for me. And tell John to tell Bur. Dim good night as of old. I have the Hair of Carroll, and Katie Safe in my knapsack. I read all of the letters I receive two or three times and then burn them. I hate to do it. But it is for the best. Has George got his letter. Tell him to shoot all the Birds he can. And Sister is not forgotten. Tell her not to trust XXX. Excuse my bad writing and spelling. And I remain Dear Mother

Your own Son
James F. Robinson

-/-/-/-/-/-/-/-/-

Flint Hill Va. Sept 23rd 1861

My Dear Brother

I was setting at my Mess Table, thinking what nice Supper, was before me. Biscuits and Preserves, out of the Box, When my name was called to get a letter. Up I jumped. I was handed your kind letter of the 17th. I was very glad to learn that all are well at home. Particularly so, because Mother had been sick with them terrible head ackes. And Father said in his last, that you had been complaining all the day before. I am glad the Horses are doing so well. I hope that you had Pedro buried. and marked so that you could find it, when I came home. For Pede has been a faithfull Dog to us, for a number of year's. I am glad to learn also that your have got such a fine dog. Do not put your heart upon any thing that I can get from the Yankee's, But if I can possible get any thing. I will remember you. You must not wait such a long time before you write again. And tell Sister that she must write too. My next will be to her. I am in the very best of health. I have increased in weight considerable. The Weather is getting quite cool here. And I am very glad of it. For it is not as sickly in Cold as in Hot Weather. I have plenty of Cloths. Tell Mother that the Cloths from Hamburg is here. And will be given out to morrow. And in my next letter she shall here from them. I find the things in the Box Splnded. Nothing broke or Spoilt. I have wrote Mother a long letter to Day. I am writing now by one of the Candles. If I have time when I return through Richmond I will try to get you some Virginia Chickens. I have told all of the new's I know. Write me soon. Do not have much to do with Gus for my sake, Dear Brother, for he is not as you all think he is. My Love to All

> God bless you all
> Your most affectionate Brother
> James F. Robinson

-/-/-/-/-/-/-

Flint Hill, Va. Oct 13th 61

Dear Father,

I have a good oppitunity of sending you a letter by hand.
And I take advantage of it. Mr. Charles Gray or as we call
him Old Uncle Charley Leaves for home again. He would not
be able to stand the Winter in this climate. I have nothing of
importance to tell you. You know more about War matter's
than I do. If there was a fight expected tomorrow I would
know nothing about. We have still some sickness in our
Company. The Regt has been on Picket for four Day's. I was
detailed as Camp Guard. They are stationed not very far
from Camp. They will be relieved to Day by Col. Cash. I
received Sister's letter of the 6th Oct. yesterday. I will answer
it in a few Days. I am sorry to hear of the Death of Wm.
Evans Jr. I have also received Papers from you. They are the
only way that I get any new's. They give me a great deel of
pleasure I can tell you. The Hat & Gloves you sent by Mr.
Gray I got safely. I found them to be splended. particular on
Guard. I am sorry that George had to lose his fine Setter. I
believe that Gus Glover was the cause of all of it. But you
have got him a Pointer just as good. I heard that C. Rodgers
could not get a discharge. The Doctor's have determined to
give no more discharges. Capt. Blodgets Company of Artillery
is at Germantown about two miles from this place. I have
not seen them but have been told that they was there. We
are going to Drill as Artillermen. I am glad of it. It will do us
no harm. and may do the greatest of good. I am glad to
learn by Sister's letter that you have made a good Crop.
Especialy Cotton & Hay. I do not suppose that you could sell
the Cotton. I am in the best of health so far. The Weather is
beginning to feel like Winter. Kiss all of the children for me.

My Love to the whole family. I remain your devoted

Son

James F. Robinson

-/-/-/-/-/-/-/-

Camp near Bull's Run Oct 17th 1861

Dear Father
    Since writing you the other few lines. Great things have
happened. The whole Army have fallen back from Flint Hill &
Fairfax to Centreville & Bull Run. We had a very trying
march of twelve miles. I have not seen the Enemy but they
say that they are advancing in great numbers. We expect a
Battle every day. Pleas write to me regular and direct as
usual Manassa. I think that if you was to put Bonham's
Brigade in one corner it would help. We are encamped to
right of where we was during the Battle. Wade Johnson has
requested me to to ask you if you see any of his folks to say
to them that he has wrote and to direct his letters as you do
mine. I am in good health. Do not be anxious about me.

Your own

Son

J.F. Robinson

-/-/-/-/-/-/-

1861
Camp near Bull's Run Oct 18th

Dear Father

I have no news to tell you. We do not expect a fight shortly. I think that we only going into Winter quarters. I send by
Mr Gray my Stud Buttons & Ristband Buttons, And may
send my Pistol if he will carry it. Write soon. The very first
chance I get I will write a long letter to Sister. My love to all
God bless you all

Your Son
James F. Robinson

-/-/-/-/-/-/-/-

Camp near Centreville, Va. Nov 15th 61

Dear Mother

The last Letter I received was from Sister. And I have also
received several packages of Papers from Father, Giving me
full and Sad accounts of the taking of Port Royal. But also
our glorious Victory in Missouri. The papers have been read
with great interest by Capt. B. crowds of privates and myself.
We have returned to our old occupation, Digging Entrenchments, prepairing for the Yankees. I paid a visit to Centreville a few days ago. From the Fortifications I could see
nothing but Tents, Horses & Guns. It seemed as if I was in
some large City. Every body was in a hurry. I could stand in
one spot all day and find amusement. On one side was the
long line of Fortifications. the Forts for Artillery and the
breastworks for Infantry. And behind them streching as far
as the Eye could reach was tents the Home of the Army of the

Potomac. In one direction I could see a Regiment drilling in double quick. And in another a Comp of Flying Artillery making the Earth tremble as they fly past. All seemed to have something they had to do quickly. Aids flying about. And then some Stern old General with his body Guard would go Staring past. their Horses feet Swords Spurs & C. rattling and rumbling. no Ladies no Children would you meet in Centreville. All Soldiers. read O. Malley, his ride from Brussel to Waterloo, his discription after or before a Battle. And you read what I see every day. The Weather is quite Cold. But as I am stirring about in the day. and have plenty of Blankets to keep me warm in the night. I do not mind it. I hear that Gen. Bonham is going to resign. We are in the divission commanded by Major Gen. Van Dorn of Texas. I have not seen him yet. It said that we will be reviewed soon and I will see him then. Some few cases of sickness. I am still in the best of health. And cannot be too thankfull to him that made me for it. My best Love to all. Do not stop writing. You do not know how I love to hear from you all. God bless you, My own Dear Mother.

Your Son,
James F. Robinson

-/-/-/-/-/-/-

Camp near Centreville Va
Sunday. Jany 5th 1862

Dear Mother

I received Fathers Letter of the 30th Dec yesterday. I am glad to hear of Fathers pleasant excursion down the River. And of the time you had during Christmas. I hope you have had a pleasant time of it on New Years day. I went to Manassas Jany 2nd with Wade Johnson to look after Boxes. By good luck both of us succeded in getting what we went after. On my way to Manassas, I passed through the Battle Grown of July 18th for the first time. Though we was in a few hundred yards of it During the Battle, yet this is the first time I have had a chance of visiting it. From the nature of the grown I could plainly see the advantage the Yankees had over our men. Not like the great Battle of the 21st. The Battle here was fought across Bull Run. On our side the bank of the Stream are low and flat with only a slight entrenchment. On the Yankees side is a high Hill. The Trees here is marred with Bullets. And the Grown on both sides of the Stream is marked with Graves. Our men was burried on our side and the Yankees on theirs. Most of our men have been dug up and carried home. The Yankees are there now except those carried away by Doctors and by those who wished to have a Yankee bone. There is a fine Bridge built across here now. On returning from Manassas we came by Mitchells Ford where we was stationed during the Battles of the 18th & 21st July 1861. I quickly recognized the Familiar place. Manassas is a small, Cold, Crowed & all together a very disagreable place. When I saw the puffing Steam Engine I looked for the Old Savannah. By accident we found one of Gen Bonhams Wagons. got our Boxes brought and a ride for ourselves. I opened my Box that Night. I opened the Bundle first and read yours and Sisters Letters. I gave Lieut Harrison Wade Johnson & Ben Neily their furs. Capt's Bland & Hard are both off. I will keep theirs until they return. I do not think you pay a very high compliment to Capt Hard, too good a marke for me, but not for him. I know you did not meen that. I found the Cake Pies Turkey Hams Cordial & C. delicious. The Georgia Scenes is great treat to me. I have often wished for a Book. We was to begin our Winter Quarters Jany 3rd went to the Grown but did nothing. We had a Storm of Sleet & Snow during the Night of Jany 3rd and we have done nothing since. The Weather is very Cold. but I have a good Chimney and I do not mind it much. I have no news to tell so I must close. A <u>Happy</u> Happy New Year to you Dear Mother

Your Son J. F. Robinson

-/-/-/-/-/-/-/-

Camp near Centreville Va
Jany 19th 1862

Dear Father

I have received your Letters regular. I received a Letter day before yesterday from Wallace Delph he requested me to remember him to you all and to say that he is still alive. he is in Camps at or near Suffolk Va. he has had better times than I have had. They are in Winter Quarters. He said that they had a large Ball on the 20th Dec. Lieut Welburn is their 2nd Lieut, John King 1st Serg, Wm. Delph 1st Corp. At the time of writing the Letter, he was rather unwell with Gout & Sore Eyes. Lieut. Col. Hamilton will be their Col. Smith Lieut. Col. and McCrady of Charleston their Maj and he thought that Rhett of the same place their Adjutant. I answered his Letter yesterday. We have begun our Winter Quarters at last. but the Weather is so bad we cannot finish them. The second day after we began we had a heavy fall of Snow, so we had to stop work. We have had Snow, Sleet & Rain ever since. it is Raining now. The Roads are wretched. teams stall with empty Wagons. but I am very comfortable. I have a good Chimney to my Tent. You mentioned about Under Shirts in your last Letter. I do not need them. I do not wear my Flannel Drawers except on Pickett. We have got used to

the Cold. And do not mind it at all. Do not send me anything more except Letters. never mind about another Box.
My time will soon be out. Capt Bland is trying to raise
another Com. he has some eaighteen (18) joined. Among
them is Wade Johnson & others. I have not signed and I am
not going to do so. If I come again it will be in another Comp.
Not that I do not like my Officers, but I do not want to come
to this part of the Southern Confederacy again. Every Capt
in the Regt is trying to get his Comp to re enlist. I have no
news to tell so I must close. Kiss all of the children for me.
God bless you Dear Father

> Your Son
> J. F. Robinson

-/-/-/-/-/-/-

> Camp near Bull Run
> Jany 27th 1862

Dear Brother

I received your note and Father's Letter of the 20th last
Night. I am very sorry you have not got my Letters regular. I
have not had the least chance to write since the 20th. We
have moved and are now building Winter Quarters Close to
the place we was stationed during the great Battle. Mr.
Chas. Gray is here. he says he has got a Letter for me. if he
has I will get it this Evening. I am in the best of Health. Do
not be anxious about me. Excuse this short Letter.

> Your Brother
> J. F. Robinson

-/-/-/-/-/-/-/-

Camp near McLane's Ford
Bull Run Feby 8th 1862

Dear Father
    I have received your kind Letters regular. This is the first chance since we moved from our Camp near Centreville. I have had of answering them. We are Encamped now between two Fords on the Bull Run. McLanes and Black-Burns. close to the Field of Battle of the 18th July. I have not yet been to the Field of the 21st yet, but will try to go the first good chance. The Men are voluntiering for the War quite fast. There are only four from our Comp. They will leave here the 10th. None in our Company that Mother or Sister is acquainted with have voluntiered. The Weather is very changeable still. there is no confidence to be placed in signs or any thing else. I have staid up at Night untill late, and when I would go to bed leave the Stars shining brightly. and get up in the Morning and find it Snowing or Raining. Ben. Neiley has returned from the Hospital I have not seen him. Wade Johnson is in the best of health. I am still in good health, and hope this miserable scrawl will find you all enjoying the same great blessing. I have not received a Letter from Mother for some time. She must spair a little time and Write me. God bless you My Dear Kind Father.
                    Your Son J.F. Robinson

-/-/-/-/-/-/-/-

Camp near Orange C.H. Va
March 24th 1862

Dear Father

I have received two Letters from you and two from Mother since I left Manassas and the banks of the Bull Run. We are now Encamped in one of the Lovliest Countries I have ever seen, And also one as true as Carolina to our Cause. We are under a very strict Officer. We have nothing to do, but are not allowed to go to any of the Houses near. Not even to burn a single Fence Rail. But we do not mind it. Col Bacon arrived here yesterday. I have not seen him yet. The Voluntiers are beginning to return to Camp. We do not expect ours untill the 1st of April. I do not all together understand the proclimations of Gov Pickens & Council. I am coming home free and foot lose. I have Just received a Package of Papers from you. I see by the Augusta Paper that quite a number of Companies is being raised there. If they will not let me Voluntier in S.C. I can in Georgia. I can see how to do when I get there. There is no talk of a Fight here now. When we was Camped near the Rappahanoc River I saw sights that made my heart feel heavy with sorrow. There is a Rail Road Bridge across the River that one can walk across but Horses and Waggons have to wade a Ford a short distance below. One day while there to draw rations, I noticed quite a number of Ladies, Young and Old. They were waiting for their Carriges & Horses to cross the Ford. They were leaving their Homes to get out of the reach of the Yankees. They were Eating their Lunch. they all seemed sad and <u>Heart</u> <u>broken</u>. They had their Servants with them. Old Men & Woman was among them.

We have no Tents and but few Blankets. On this March I experience what I never thought of doing. that is a long and continued March. The first day my knapsack did not hurt me untill I reached Manassas. before starting we was ordered to Cook three days rations, but we did not start untill late in the Evening of the Second day after the Wagons left us. therefore we was nearly out of Provissions. and a three days March a head of us before we would get up with the Wagons. While we was at Manassas we got two Hams. I had to carry one of them in my Haversack, it weighed about twelve pounds. I could not keep up after that. I dropped behind and Slep in the Woods. The Evening of the Second day of our March I came in sight of the Regt encamped for the Night, thinking I might be put on Guard if I went to them, I stopped in a barn only a quarter of a mile behind them. I went up stairs there I found a (Hen Nest) with seventeen (17) Eggs in it. My Hands stuck to them so fast I had to take them. I had brought with me from Camp a light Coffee boiler tied to my knapsac. We had a fine Supper that Night I can tell you. But the Cream of the Joke is that Major Seibels was under me when I took them, but he knows nothing as yet. I caught up with the Regt the next day and kept up with them untill we Camped in this place. I have no news to tell you so I must close this poor Letter. Hoping to be with you all soon. Kiss all of the Children for me not excepting Mifs Anna, Maude or Matilda Robinson. God bless you my Dear Father.

> Your Son
> J.F. Robinson

or Barnum as my Mess calls me

-/-/-/-/-/-/-/-

> Camp on Chickahominy River
> near Richmond Va. June 11th 62

My Dear Father

    I have not received a Letter from you for sometime, but I know the reason why. Mother said in her last Letter that you had gone to North Carolina on buisness. I was in great hopes that you could prolong your journey and come to Richmond. I saw Mr Hard one day last week. he said that he saw you and that you made him promise to Telegraph you. I asked him to let me pay for it but he said that you and him would settle it and I said no more about it. afraid I might hurt his feelings by ensisting on Paying for it. I received the Papers and Letter & C you sent me. I would like to hear from you very much and also oftener from all the rest of the family. Our Regt was not in the Fight here on the 31st May & 1st June. We reached the Field too late in the night to engage in the Fight. We are now taking things cool and Easy. we go on Picquett twice a Week. the remainder of the time we spend in Drilling, Working, Eating, Sleeping & watching the movements of the Enemy. We are Encamped within a hundred and fifty yards of our Picquett line, wich is about six hundred yards from the Yankees Picquets. They throw Shot & Shell every day far over our Camp. We have here a very good position. Oh to God that they would attempt to take by the point of the Bayonet, We would learn them something. The S. Carolina Troops gained high Honer in the last Fight. The Northern account gives them more credit than ours do. Look out for Kershaw's Brigade, we will make our mark yet, if old Stone Wall dont scare them too much. As yesterdays Richmond Dispatch say's he has another Victory, and that over Shield's. The Weather here is very changeful. Sometimes Hot and sometimes Cold and a great deal more Rain than is pleasant to us Soldiers. I see from S. C. quite a number. among them Julius Day & Wm Spires from our neighborhood. Mr Timmerman from Edge Dist. & a Mr DeBurt from Abberville, and also Mr Hard. I expect you know them all. I have seen several of Pick, Butlers Co, among them Wm Remighan, Casper Gardner & Wm Delph. They are all in fine health and say's that the rest are also, except John King who is their 3rd Lieut and is sick in Richmond but only slightly. William Told me to remember him to you, Mother & all the

Family. I have not seen Wallace yet but he is Sergt Major of the Regt. I know you will be glad to hear of his promotion. Capt Harrison says that Wallace is the Hansomest young Man he knows of. P. O. Ransom is also in good health. I have not saw him eaither since I have been Orderly. I have had no time to spair, but I will go to see them the very first chance I have. I have not seen Harrison Butler lately but heard that he is in good health. Wade Johnson is still homouraass as ever and allways keeps his maxem of Free & Easy. I have no more news to tell. Everything is quiet. All expecting a Fight every Day & Night. I am still enjoying the greatest blessing bestowed upon Man that is good Health. And I hope and pray that these few lines may You and all the rest of the loved ones enjoying the same. And that God may bless you, My own Dear Father is the Prayer of

Your Son
James F. Robinson

P.S. Lieut. Welborn is also well.

J.F.R.

-/-/-/-/-/-/-

Camp near the York Riddle R.R. June 15/62

My Dear Mother

I have not received a Letter from any of you for allmost two Weeks. what can the matter be. the Mails come and go regular. I write regular but do not receive any. I saw Mr R. J. Butler yesterday, he came over to our Camp expressly to see me. Harrison is quite unwell and Mr Butler is trying him a short Furlough to go home. He speaks quite hard of Mr

Spires who came to Virginia and quite close to Harrison and did not attempt to see him. I only met him by accident. I am also glad to hear that you all have such a good crop. Mr. Butler showed me some Leather he had Tanned. it looked very well. He says he will have four thousand bushels of Peaches. He did not stay long. He wanted to start for home that day. The Weather is very warm. We are Drilling. Working & other duties of a Soldiers Life. We are taking things easy. we have moved near the York River Rail Road. I went to see the boys of Picks Butler's Comp. I am sorry to hear that Capt Butler has some children very Sick. I saw all the boy's from Hamburg. They all look fine. they have a very good uniform. Lieut Welborn and all of the boy's send their best respects to Father & all of you. I have no news to write. It is so Hot I must close this short & poor Letter. You all must write more than you do. I am still in good health, And I hope these few lines may find you all enjoying the same great Blessing. God bless you my own Dear Mother.

> Your Son
> James F. Robinson

-/-/-/-/-/-/-/-

Camp Reserve, near Richmond, Va
July 27th 1862

My Dear Father

I received your Letter of the 18th July 62 a few days ago. It is the first and only letter I have received from Home dated since the Battle. I wonder the reason. not a line from Mother, Sister, Brother or any except you. I am glad to hear that all are well at Home. Crops fine & Fruit plenty. I am getting on fine. the Weather warm. Duty quite light. Vegitables getting cheaper. Fruit coming in very fast. Have you all ever received the Ambrotypes. you will not let me know wether you did or not. the Regt is in fine health. very few sick cases. Tell Pulaskie that Wm Powell & Power Huckelby is in our Regt Comp. D from Abberville. I had a long talk with W. Power the 2nd July the day after the Battle. I sent a message to be Telegraphed to you in Augusta by Sergt Huiet. he either saw you or heard that you had Telegraphed home so he did not Telegraph. I am glad to hear that Harrison Butler has arrived Home safe. Wade Johnson is in fine health. he got a Letter from Mrs Larneir his Sister. he told me about it. the Letter mentioned that Jack Kennady had lost his youngest son in Richmond. I suppose it was Joe. I was very sorry to hear it. Please give my best respects to Jolly Kennedy & his wife & the Vandeveers & also to Jack & Mrs. Kennedy & all of their family especialy to poor Wat. I hope he is getting well. Col Aiken has received your Letter. he told me about it, he has not the power even to sign his name. I do not expect a Furlough untill Winter. I have no news to write so you must excuse my short & poor Letter, but Write oftener I do so long to hear from you all. I am in good health & fine spirits. God bless you my Dear Father.

Your Son
James F. Robinson

-/-/-/-/-/-/-

Camp near Drury's Bluff, Va
Aug 12th 1862

Dear Mother
    I have received four Letters from you & Sister lately, two dated 1st and two dated 6th Aug. This is the very first

chance I have had of answering them. We have been moving every day since my last Letter. Hot as the Weather is we have had to march 15 miles We are now Encamped near Drury's Bluff on James River. I have not received my Bundle yet and I think never will. you all ought never to Send any thing by a Soldier. Fleming's Regt is with Jackson, The Conscripts for our Regt has arrived at last. We have got 44 in our Comp. I have my hands full now I can assure you. They are a fine looking Set of Men. I only knew one William Harlin from Hamburg. he staid at Bill Hill's store. The Regt has gone to Malverne's Hill. it is reported that the Yankees have taken it. by a especial order of the Col's I am left behind to drill the recruits. quite a compliment, saved me from a hard march. I have received your scolding Letter. read & reread it. Dear Mother your Letter plainly shows me some things, among them, your love for me, and also you imperfect knowledge of Millitary Life. I will relate a circumstance to show. W. D. Mims poor fellow a gallant Soldier, got wounded in fight on Malvern's Hill. the Ball lodging between the bones above the wrist. the wound was considered a slight one. he was sent to Richmond where his arm was cut off. a negro belonging the Comp (Harrison's) went to the City for things for his master, He saw the poor fellow lying off by himself, who begged him for God's sake to stay with him untill Night. to keep the Flies from eating him up. he did so. when the negro returned he was asked what kept him. he told what he had done. that Night Capt Harrison went to see the Col to let one of Mims Cousens, he has two in the Comp, go to wait on him. he told the Col that Mims would die if he did not have better attendance, the Col would not let even one go. a few day's after Mims died. I was well acquainted with him. Please excuse my poor & short Letter. I have so much to do that I can not write oftener. But remember my whole Heart is with & for you. God bless my Dear Mother.

Your devoted Son
J. F. Robinson

REMEMBER ME

-/-/-/-/-/-/-/-

Culpepper C.H. Va,
Sept. 23, 1862

Mr. George Robinson - My Dear Sir:

It grives me to tell you that your son, Sergt. James F. Robinson has fallen; he was killed on Maryland Heights, on the 13th, while charging the enemy. He was struck in the forehead, and expired with out uttering a word. Let it be a consolation to you that he died amidst the victorious shouts of his comrades, whilst facing the enemy in the performance of his duty. He was as brave as he was efficient, and his uniformly courteous behavior and gentleness of manners were remarked by the Colonel. Let us hope, as we certainly have reason for hoping, that from those lofty heights his spirit took its course heavenward - exchanging the shock, the shout, the groan of war, for the bright word of peace and bliss.

> "Now lies he low - no more to hear
> The victor's shout or crashing steel:
> No more of war's rude cares to bear,
> No more kind sympathy to feel.
> No more he charges with the host
> The thickest of the battle field,
> No more to join in victory's boast,
> No more to see the vanquished yield".

Yours Truly,
H. W. Addison

J.F.R. OBITUARY

Another Youthful Hero Gone

Our fellow citizen, Mr. George Robinson, has the sympathies of numerous friends in the loss of his gallant boy, who, having been among the first in the land to grasp his musket and having promptly braved a thousand perils, has at length fallen at the front of battle. The fallowing tribute is from his commanding officer:

Culpepper C. H., Va., Sept. 23, 1862

Mr. Geo. Robinson--*My Dear Sir:*

It grieves me to tell you that your son, Serg't Jas. F. Robinson, has fallen; he was killed while charging the enemy. He was struck in the forehead, and expired without uttering a word. Let it be a consolation to you that he died amidst the victorious shouts of his comrades, whilst facing the enemy in the performance of his duty. He was brave as he was efficient, and his uniformly courteous behaviour and gentleness of manners were even remarked by the Colonel. Let us hope as we certainly have reason for hoping, that from those lofty heights his spirit took its course heavenward--exchanging the shock, the shout, the groan of war, for the bright world of peace and bliss.

"Now lies he low--no more to hear
The victor's shout or clashing steel;
No more of war's rude cares to bear,
No more kind sympathy to feel.
No more he charges with the host
The thickest of the battle-field,
No more to join in victory's boast'
No more to see the vanquished yield."

Yours truly,
H. W. Addison

This brave youth (he was but a boy when the war opened) was among the earliest volunteers in South Carolina,--was at Charleston among the first who hastened at the tap of the Palmetto drum, and has been ever since in active service. Let his fond parents yield their child to his country and his God with resignation not unmingled with satisfaction. His name is on the Roll of Honor upon earth,--let us trust it is also on the Roll of the Redeemed above.

TRIBUTE

IN MEMORY
OF
Sergeant James F. Robinson.

Mr. Editor: Allow a friend and comrade to pay a last sad tribute to the memory of the youthful martyr whose name stands mournfully at the head of this brief eulogy.

Sergeant Robinson's fall, while glorious to himself as a hero and patriot, was one of the severest blows of this cruel war upon the home alters of affection and friendship. To his immediate family it was as heart-rending as it was sudden; but scarcely less afflicting was that melancholy event to the friends and brothers-in-arms who had known him, a true man and a whole-souled soldier, in all the varied experience of camp-life and camp-duties, and who had witnessed with admiration his lofty bearing upon the blood-stained battle fields of old Virginia.

Sergeant James F. Robinson left the bosom of his devoted family early in '61, and, full of enthusiasm in the good cause of Southern Independence, joined the 1st South Carolina Regiment, Col. Maxey Gregg, and was amongst the heroic few who participated in the Battle of Fort Sumter, the first scene in the drama of this mighty war. He afterwards joined the 7th S. C. V., Col. Thomas G. Bacon, and remained with it until the day of his death. Having borne his part in the battles before Richmond, he answered to the roll-call when the army entered Maryland, and was ever at his post of duty in that campaign up to the fatal 13th September 1862. On that day, while the soldiers of the South were rendering the name of Maryland Heights immortal in story, he fell in the desperate onset, and fell, alas! to rise no more.

And what shall I say of him, commensurate with his valor and unwavering devotion to duty? If there was a man in the Southern ranks who completely denied self and lent his efforts wholly to the promotion of the comfort of those around him and to the onward movement of our good cause, this youth, this boy was that man. Kind, attentive, active, industrious, cheerful and genial, he was ever uplifting his comrades by hopeful words and pleasant acts. It is indeed to such spirits as his, acting sympathetically upon hearts drawn to them amid the toils of war, that our army owes much of its already world-wide renown. But our gallant brother, our beloved friend is no more. He is gone from us, never to return. Yet, while memory lives and the Old Seventh has one beating heart left to recall the campaigns of Virginia, the word of affection will rise to the lips and the tear of regret will start to the eye at the mention of the name of James F. Robinson.

It may be proper to add that the deceased fell in the charge upon the second abattis at Maryland Heights. He breathed but a moment after he was shot, and uttered not a word nor heaved a single sigh. He was buried by the men of his Regiment. The spot where we laid him is remembered; and it will be easy to recover his remains when the vicessitudes of the war will permit. We turn away from this unworthy tribute as we did from his distant, solitary grave, with the words farewell, farewell, still dwelling on our lips and sinking into our souls.

ONE OF THE BOYS